Other Books

Over The Hedge

Also by Michael Fry

What I Want to Be When THEY Grow Up
The First Collection of *Committed*

OVER THE HEDGE 2

by Michael Fry and T Lewis

Andrews and McMeel
A Universal Press Syndicate Company
Kansas City

T Lewis and Michael Fry:
Excerpts from a Swedish on-line chat session 9/9/96

Torbjörn: Hi. Who does the translation of your comics into Swedish? Do you think it is as funny as it is in English?

T Lewis: I don't know who does the translation . . . the syndicate (the company that distributes the comic) handles that. You'll have to judge if it's funny in Swedish. Sometimes after working for a long time on a strip, I can't even tell if it's funny in English!

Michael Fry: I think the translation is hysterical, but then I don't speak Swedish.

Peo: Is it difficult being two guys? Who does what?

Michael Fry: Being two people is always tough. Who gets to hold the pen? Who gets to spend the money? It's always a struggle.

Esset: What do you know about Sweden?

T Lewis: I've had a crush on Liv Ullman for twenty years.

Michael Fry: I understand it's pretty dark a good portion of the year and there are a lot of blonds. I'm not sure these concepts are related though. Oh, and you end all your statements like a question. How's that for all the stereotypes?

Host: Where are you guys?

T Lewis: I'm in a small town in eastern Washington State. . . . Mike is about 1700 miles away in Houston, Texas.

Michael Fry: I live in Houston, but my family and I are moving to Austin to become one with our more cowboy side.

TT: Are you against byrocrasy?

T Lewis: Whenever I get against anything, I get a rash.

Michael Fry: Byrocasy? Sounds like an intestinal parasite. . . . Is it contagious?

TT: Is it easier to make comics with animals in them?

Michael Fry: Well, animals never make unreasonable contract demands. Actually, they don't make any contract demands.

T Lewis: You can focus on things with animals that you cannot with people, because they are innocent outsiders. They also cross racial and cultural boundaries (as this interview points out).

Michael Fry: I'm pretty sure Verne is Finnish, but we don't like to let that get around.

Mattias: Why did you choose these characters? Why not a cow and a snake?

T Lewis: MIKE!!! I TOLD YOU WE SHOULD HAVE USED A COW AND A SNAKE!!!

Michael Fry: Disney has sewed up all the rights to cows and snakes. Damn that Michael Eisner!

Erland J: Liv Ullman is Norwegian.

T Lewis: How could anyone that beautiful and cultured NOT be from Sweden???

Michael Fry: I knew Liv was Norwegian.

Mattias: When did you come up with the idea about "livet I häcken?"

Michael Fry: We were going to do a strip about pigs, but nobody felt that pigs had any commercial potential, except of course until the movie *Babe* came out and now everyone's into pigs. So we went for a turtle and a raccoon. Hey, are there raccoons in Sweden?

Host: Michael, I don't think we have any, sad enough!

Mattias: No, there are neither turtles nor raccoons in Sweden. But there are some moose.

Michael Fry: No turtles! This is terrible. I could have sworn there was such a thing as snow turtles.

Iggy: I guess that writing a comic strip is kind of the same thing as trying to become a rock star . . . many try it, but just a few make it . . . how long did you try before you could make a living at it? Sorry for my slow computer . . .

Michael Fry: I've been at it for seventeen years. Before that I was a very successful rock star. Cartooning is much more difficult.

Iggy: I am allergic to animals. Do you think it's safe for me to read "live over the hedge?"

T Lewis: I suggest that Iggy read the strip only after taking the precaution of sitting in a tub of yeast extract.

Michael Fry: With the combined use of various medications, it is now possible to read *Over the Hedge* without fear of sneezing, coughing, or that over-all achey feeling. But please don't operate any heavy machinery . . .

Träd K. Ramare: Have you ever been harassed by animal rights groups?

Michael Fry: Well, no. Why, don't they bathe?

Johan: Are your strips tested on animals? I mean, are they approved by the Animal Liberation Movement?

Michael Fry: No animals were harmed in the making of this comic strip. Verne claims to have ripped a hang-nail, but our lawyers have advised us not to comment on the matter.

T Lewis: No animals were harmed during the drawing of the strip. There is some radioactivity produced, but so far it just seems to make mice rock back and forth, with little smiles on their little faces.

Bo A Orm: How are you coming up with the ideas for everything? By the way, do you know what the swedish word "helballt" means?

T Lewis: I believe it translates as "pardon me, you're standing on my pants."

Michael Fry: We buy all our ideas on the black market. Helballt? Some sort of fermented yak fat?

Mattias: I saw your comic in the small newspaper *Smalänningen*. *Smalänningen* is a local newspaper in Ljungby.

T Lewis: Seriously . . . what does "helballt" mean?

Bo A Orm: Helballt means real cool.

Iggy: . . . or real groovy

Michael Fry: A vowel! My kingdom for a vowel!

T Lewis: I now love Ljungby. I'm going to name my second child Ljungby. I just love the sound of it . . . Ljungby Ljungby Ljungby Ljungby!

Vincent: Do you prefer Donald Duck or Mickey Mouse?

T Lewis: Ljungby Ljungby Ljungby . . . oh, sorry . . . Well, I prefer Mickey in a sweet wine sauce. But Donald flambe is not bad.

T Lewis: To really answer the Mickey question: I prefer Donald, although I drew Mickey Mouse for two years. He is lots of fun to draw (difficult, though).

Johan: Helballt=Far out man; cool. Now you know four swedish words (besides moped, ombudsman, and smorgosbord).

Michael Fry: Moped is not Swedish. C'mon . . .

tobb: T, you did draw Mickey Mouse for a while; is that correct?

T Lewis: Yes, I did Mickey for about two years for King Features who had an agreement with Disney to produce the strip.

Michael Fry: Hey, I wrote Mickey for a few years too. What I would do is drink a liter of vodka and bang my head against the wall for twenty minutes and then, "presto," I became Mickey!

Iggy: OK, my last one is just a simple thank you for making me laugh and good luck in the future . . . and don't forget that I will read your work one im hardly awake so keep on make me laugh to counciouness (and I don't know how to spell it:o))

T Lewis: Thanks everybody . . . don't let your kids grow up to be artists . . .

YOU'VE BEEN LISTENING TO THE DR. VLAD RAPTOR SHOW, AMERICA'S FAVORITE GRIM REALIST...

...DON'T FORGET TO ORDER DR. VLAD'S BOOK OF DAILY AFFIRMATIONS...

FRY. LEWIS

...OPERATORS ARE STANDING BY...

"YOU CAN ATTRACT MORE SHARKS WITH CHUM"?

"FLASH THE OTHER CHEEK"?

LET A SCOWL BE YOUR FLAK JACKET
DR. VLAD RAPTOR

R.J., I'VE GOT AN ETHICAL DILEMMA FOR YOU.

SHOOT.

IF YOU FOUND A TWINKIE ON THE GROUND, WOULD YOU EAT IT...OR TRY TO FIND ITS RIGHTFUL OWNER?

HMMM...

WAK!

FRY. LEWIS

KOW!

...I'D WANT TO SPARE THE OWNER THE *PUBLIC HUMILIATION* RESULTING FROM SUCH A CASUAL DISREGARD OF *TWINKIE SANCTITY.*

SO, IT WOULD BE SELFISH OF YOU *NOT* TO EAT IT.

DIGEST BEFORE DISHONOR.

YOU'RE NUTS IF YOU THINK CHICKS DIG THIS STUFF.

SHH... ‡AHEM‡

"MY LOVE IS LIKE A RED, RED NOSE..."

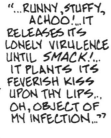

"...RUNNY, STUFFY, ACHOO!...IT RELEASES ITS LONELY VIRULENCE UNTIL SMACK!... IT PLANTS ITS FEVERISH KISS UPON THY LIPS... OH, OBJECT OF MY INFECTION..."

"MY LOVE IS LIKE A RED, RED NOSE."

HOW WAS THAT?

THEY FOUND IT QUITE MOVING.

NATE!!!...DID YOU READ THE DIRECTIONS ON THE FERTILIZER?!

OF COURSE... WHAT'S THE....

WELL, I'M IMPRESSED, VERNE.

...YAAAAAAAA!!!

YEAH, IT'S AMAZING WHAT YOU CAN DO WITH LEFTOVER MASHED POTATOES AND WET NEWSPAPERS.

18

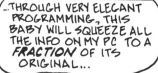

23

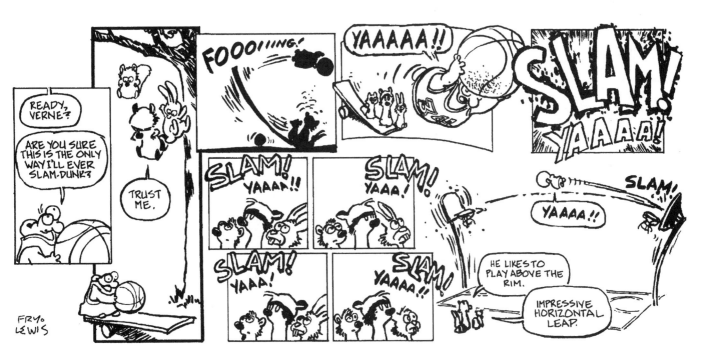

VERNE, WHAT DO YOU THINK OF MY BOLD NEW ARCHITECTURAL CREATION?

HOMEY, HOWARD.

I WAS GOING FOR A SORT OF "FRANK LLOYD WRIGHT MEETS MIKE BRADY"

FRY LEWIS

THAT EXPLAINS THE SUNKEN LIVING ROOM.

FRY LEWIS

HOWARD, YOU'VE GOT A MIGHTY FINE DAM HERE.

DAM?!

ANY FOOL CAN THROW A FEW MILLION TONS OF CONCRETE IN THE WAY OF A SILLY LITTLE RIVER!

IT TAKES VISION TO WEAVE STICKS AND MUD INTO A SOLID MASS STRONG ENOUGH TO WITHSTAND THE FORCES OF NATURE!!... IT TAKES ART!!

HMM... "FORM FLOODS FUNCTION."

HAND ME SOME MORE DUCT TAPE, WILL YOU?

R.J., I'M CONCERNED THAT PLUSHIE ISN'T GETTING ENOUGH EXCERCISE.

CLICK!

CLICK!

CLICK!

CLICK!

WELL, HIS HAND-FOOT-TONGUE-NOSE-EYE COORDINATION SEEMS TO BE IN PRETTY GOOD SHAPE!

NICE HEAD BUTT.

CLICK!

I JUST WONDER IF PLUSHIE'S GOING TO TURN OUT OK.

VERNE, WHEN I WAS SHORT, DAD WOULD SIT ME IN FRONT OF OUR 19" SYLVANIA AND SAY "WATCH OR WANE."

AND LOOK AT ME TODAY!

BRAIN-DEAD.

ISN'T IT GREAT? NOW I HAVE A PLACE TO PUT MY HANKIE!

THE PROBLEM IS THAT PLUSHIE ISN'T *GAINING* ANYTHING FROM TV!

OH, BUNK, ANXIOUS-BOY.

HIT IT, PLUSHIE!

SIR ISAAC NEWTON DISCOVERED GRAVITY WHEN AN APPLE WAS DROPPED ON HIS HEAD...

SEE?

DROPPED?

...BY MR. PEABODY AND SHERMAN.

WEEKDAYS ON THE LEARNING CHANNEL.

45

I CAN'T TELL WHICH WAY THIS IS GOING TO BREAK.

HMM... LEFT, THEN RIGHT... THEN DOWN THE HILL, THEN OFF THE MOUND AND A LEFT HAIRPIN AT THE HOLE.

FRY·LEWIS

PLIP!

OO... OO...

EEE...

PLOOP!

YESS!

THIS EXIT

YOU JUST HAVE TO BE ABLE TO READ THE GREENS.

CAUTION

DIP

SO... WHAT DO I OWE YOU?

FRY·LEWIS

WELL, WE STARTED PLAYING AT A NICKEL A HOLE... THEN YOU PRESSED AND DOUBLE-PRESSED AND TRIPLE-PRESSED AND QUADRUPLE-PRESSED AND... AND...

YOU OWE ME # 4,345,985.35

WHAT?! THAT CAN'T BE RIGHT!!

OH, YEAH... I FORGOT TO SUBTRACT 75¢ FOR THE FRESCA YOU BOUGHT ME ON 14.

THOUGHT I WASN'T PAYING ATTENTION, DIDN'T YA?

50

HMM... WHAT WOULD YOU THINK OF THAT LOG IN MORE OF A "MYSTIC SEAPORT SUNRISE ROSE AMBER"?

¿COMO?

IT'S HER LINE OF DESIGNER COLORS FOR HABITAT IMPROVEMENT!

WHAT?!...

...SHE THINKS SHE CAN COMPETE WITH MOTHER NATURE?!

DON'T BE SILLY... SHE'S NOT THAT PRESUMPTUOUS!...

FRY LEWIS

...THEY MERGED.

"MOTHER STEWART, INC."?

53

WHEN THIS HI-TECH LIFE GETS TOO INTENSE... IT'S A COMFORT TO KNOW SOME THINGS ARE BEYOND SCIENTIFIC UNDERSTANDING...

...BEAUTY, FOR INSTANCE.

FRY. LEWIS

BUT, VERNE, OLD POOP, THEY'VE GOT THAT *ALL* FIGURED OUT...

IT'S JUST NEUROCHEMICALS REACTING TO EXTERNAL STIMULI!

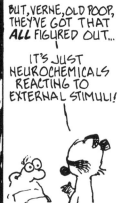

≡SIGH≡

RELAX... THEY STILL DON'T KNOW WHAT'S IN A TWINKIE!

VERNE... DO YOU SOMETIMES YEARN FOR A SIMPLER TIME?...

OFTEN...

...IT'D BE NICE TO RETURN TO THE DAYS WHEN THERE WERE ONLY 48 CHANNELS... THE WEB WAS LARGELY POPULATED BY PREENING CYBER-TROLLS AND A MEG OF RAM STILL COST $500...

...WHEN BEING A TECHIE CONFERRED SOME *STATUS.*

FRY. LEWIS

BEFORE AMERICA ONLINE.

THERE WENT THE NEIGHBORHOOD.

61

BEHOLD...THE PERFECT MELDING OF *NEIGHBORS* AND *NATURE!*

A MASTER-PLANNED COHABITAT?

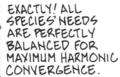

EXACTLY! ALL SPECIES' NEEDS ARE PERFECTLY BALANCED FOR MAXIMUM HARMONIC CONVERGENCE.

TWO DOZEN STAGNANT REST PUDDLES?

NOT ENOUGH?

LET ME SEE THAT PROSPECTUS.

"WELCOME TO *TURTOPIA*"?!

I *COULD* ADD SOME MORE "WADE-UP WETLAND BARS..."

AS YOU CAN SEE... EVERYTHING IN *TURTOPIA* IS WITHIN EASY WALKING, FLYING OR CRAWLING DISTANCE.

TURTOPIA
A MASTER-PLANNED
COHABITAT FOR
ALL SPECIES

PIZZA HUT, 7-ELEVEN, BLOCKBUSTER... HMM...WHAT'S THAT OVER THERE BY STARBUCKS?

GREEN SPACE.

VERNE... LOSE THAT AND YOU SHORTEN MY COMMUTE TO BEN & JERRY'S BY NEARLY 20 SECONDS.

THEN WHERE WOULD WE HOLD THE ANNUAL "BLADE-CAPADES"?

IN THE "OLD NAVY" PARKING LOT.

WHAT MAKES YOU THINK PEOPLE WILL GO FOR YOUR TURTOPIAN CONCEPT?

LOOK... THEY WANT TO BE CLOSE TO NATURE... BUT NOT *TOO* CLOSE...

TURTOPIA
THE MASTER-PLANNED
COHABITAT FOR
ALL SPECIES

"...WE GIVE THEM WHAT *THEY* WANT..."

"TASTEFUL, REGULARLY SCHEDULED FORAGING WITH RANDOM DISPLAYS OF ADORABLENESS"

TURTOPIA
DREAM
THE
DREAM

...AND *WE* GET WHAT *WE* WANT!

"...FREE DIGITAL, SATELLITE ACCESS TO THE 24-HOUR 'ALL XENA—ALL THE TIME' NETWORK."

FRY·LEWIS

REALLY GLANCING DOWN.

LOOK, IT'S A WASTE OF TIME... YOU'RE *NOT* GOING TO GET ME INTERESTED IN THE USENET!

M FRY O T LEWIS

HMMM... "ALT. SNACKCAKES. DINGDONGS. CREAMFILLING. SECRETRECIPE!"

TELL ME YOU'VE GOT A PINCH OF *POLYSORBATE 60*!!

LET ME CHECK MY CHEMISTRY SET.

I JUST WANT TO BE SURGICALLY ATTACHED TO THAT "SLUSHEE" NOZZLE, AND LET MY GUT RUNNETH OVER!

YOU'RE DISGUSTING.

7 to 11 MINI-MARKET

I JUST SAY OUT LOUD WHAT EVERYBODY'S THINKING!

I WASN'T THINKING THAT.

PUSH

NO... YOU WANT TO DO A SWAN DIVE INTO THE PICKLED-EGG JAR AND SNORKLE AMONGST THE YOLKS.

YOU'RE SO FAR OFF... YOU DON'T KNOW ME AT ALL.

...A DOUBLE TWISTING HALF-GAINER IN THE PIKE POSITION.

FRY O LEWIS

LUCKY GUESS!!

EUREKA!... AN EXPIRED BOX OF "SLIM JIMS"!...

FRY • LEWIS

...WE'VE HIT THE MOTHER LODE, R.J.! ...R.J.?

NUMBER 23... "YOU EXECUTE YOUR MATING DANCE TO THE: A) BEE GEES... B) CHIPMUNKS... C) THEME FROM 'MR. BELVEDERE'... D) 'RADAR LOVE'...

WILL YOU PUT DOWN THAT "WOODSMOPOLITAN" AND HELP ME OUT?!!

CHILL!... I'M TAKING THE "WHAT'S YOUR RUTTING I.Q.?" TEST...

"I'VE BEEN DRIVIN' ALL NIGHT, MY HAND'S WET ON THE WHEEL" ...DO, DO-DO, DO-DO ...DOOOO...

THIS IS THE LIFE... A MOONLIGHT SWIM... A JUG OF MOUNTAIN DEW... AND TAO!...

...VERNE, OLD POOP, IT DOESN'T GET ANY BETTER'N THIS!

FRY • LEWIS

YOU KNOW WHAT? YOU'RE RIGHT!!!

...THIS IS IT! THE BEST!!...

...IT'S ALL JUST DOWNHILL FROM HERE!!!

OKAY... WILL YOU RELAX?!... I RETRACT THE OBSERVATION... IT CAN ALWAYS BE BETTER.

HOW?!

THE 'DEW IS FLAT.

WHEW!... FOR A SECOND THERE I THOUGHT I HAD NOTHING TO LIVE FOR!

70

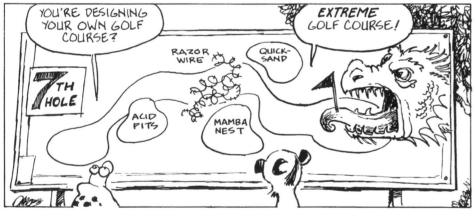

NO ONE'S GOING TO WANT TO PLAY YOUR *EXTREME GOLF COURSE.*

HOLE 18 PAR 666

SURE THEY WILL...

...IF...

...THEY HAVE THE *RIGHT CLUBS!*

EXTRA WIDE SWEET-SPOT?

FOR GETTING PAST THOSE PESKY, GIANT, BLOOD-SUCKING WEREPOODLES ON #14.

FRYOLEWIS

76

VERNE, TELL ME WHAT IT WAS LIKE NOT TO MAKE THE *OLYMPIC TWISTER* TEAM...

I WAS DEVASTATED, JIM...

IT WAS THE FINAL ROUND... THE CALL WAS "LEFT FOOT, GREEN"... A MOVE I'VE MADE A MILLION TIMES... I REACHED... AND *DISASTER* STRUCK!

FRY. LEWIS

HAMSTRING PULL?

WELL, I'M A LITTLE EMBAR...

BLADDER CRAMP.

NATURE SUMMONED?

I *TOLD* YOU TO DISCONNECT CALL WAITING!

ONCE AGAIN... IT'S AN ALL-CHINESE OLYMPIC TWISTER FINAL!...

SOMETHING'S ROTTEN IN THE STATE OF MANCHURIA...

THEY'RE *TOO GOOD!*

RIGHT FOOT... *RED!* LEFT FOOT... *BLUE!* RIGHT HAND... *GREEN!*

OOO... NICE MOVE!

THERE'S ONLY ONE OLYMPIC TWISTONIAN WHO CAN SCULPT HIS LEGS INTO A DOUBLE HELIX!!

FRY • LEWIS

GHUM BI?!

I DIDN'T KNOW HE DEFECTED!

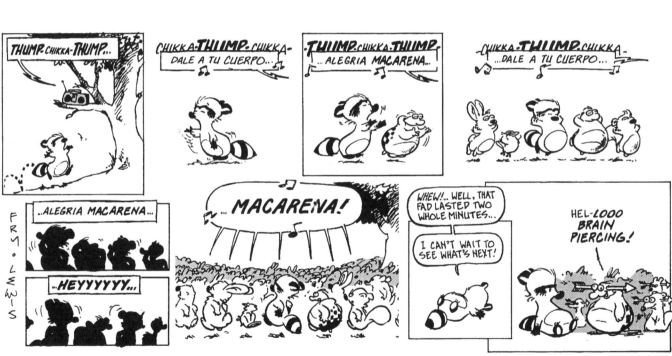

R.J., I'M WORRIED ABOUT PLUSHIE.

HEY... HE'S *ACES*, SAMURAI WORRIER.

BUT AS HIS UNCLE, IT'S MY RESPONSIBILITY TO MAKE SURE HE DEVELOPS A *MORAL CENTER*.

HMM... NO...NO...

...LOOKS MORE LIKE CHEWY NOUGAT TO ME!

PLUSHIE, DO YOU KNOW WHAT A CONSCIENCE IS?

UNCLE VERNE, IT'S THAT VOICE IN MY HEAD TELLING ME RIGHT FROM WRONG.

AND DO YOU *LISTEN* TO THAT VOICE?

NO...

...R.J. UNPLUGGED IT.

WHAT?!

...TOO MUCH "ANNOYING FEEDBACK."

NAG, NAG, NAG, ALL DAY LONG.

I CAN'T *BELIEVE* YOU'D TRY TO SILENCE PLUSHIE'S *CONSCIENCE!*

YOU'RE SO CUTE WHEN YOU'RE CONVULSING...

...VERNE... MORALITY DOESN'T COME FROM A LITTLE VOICE IN YOUR *HEAD*... IT'S A DIRECT PROJECTION OF A *CONSCIOUS CHOICE* TO BE TRUE TO THE BEST *WITHIN YOURSELF!*

FRY LEWIS

HAVE YOU BEEN READING AGAIN?

BAZOOKA JOE'S BEEN KINDA PHILOSOPHICAL LATELY.

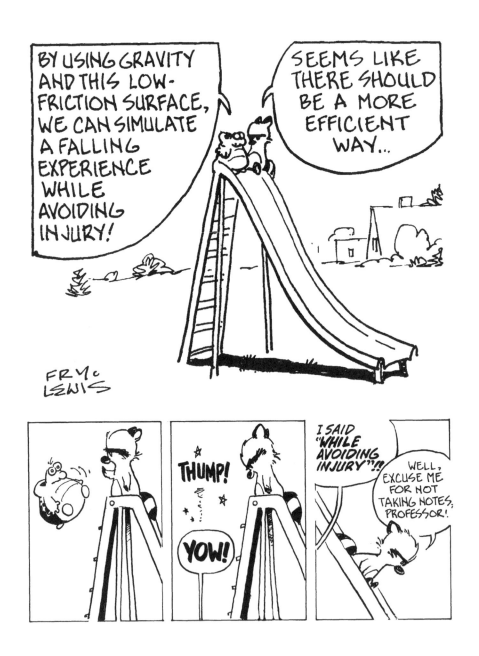

86

91

DO YOU THINK I SHOULD ASK VELMA OUT?

DIDN'T SHE SAY SHE WOULD RATHER HAVE HER SPLEEN REMOVED WITHOUT ANESTHESIA THAN GO OUT WITH YOU AGAIN?

FRY. LEWIS

BUT WHAT DOES *THAT* MEAN?

"NO," VERNE.

WELL, WHY CAN'T SHE JUST *SAY THAT*?!!

SHE WOULDN'T WANT TO HURT YOUR FEELINGS.

I HAVE THIS STRANGE EFFECT ON THE OPPOSITE SEX, R.J.

NAUSEA?

YEAH! EXACTLY!

TOO MUCH SWOONING.

FRY.LEWIS

THAT'S WHAT *I* WAS THINKING!

VERNE...THEY LOSE THEIR EQUILIBRIUM IN YOUR PRESENCE.

YOU'RE SAYING I SHOULD LAY OFF THE CHARM?

AND THE OLD SPICE.

R.J...DO YOU EVER WONDER WHY WE HAVE THIS ODD ATTRACTION TO FEMALES?

I MEAN...IT MUST BE SOME *INSTINCTUAL* WAY TO BRING US TOGETHER...

...TO DO SOMETHING FOR *EACH OTHER* THAT WE CAN'T DO *ALONE*.

FRY. LEWIS

BACK RUBS.

SURE!...THAT WORKS FOR *US*, BUT WHAT DO *THEY* GET OUT OF IT?!

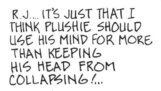

R.J.... IT'S JUST THAT I THINK PLUSHIE SHOULD USE HIS MIND FOR MORE THAN KEEPING HIS HEAD FROM COLLAPSING!...

... I WANT HIM TO *THINK!*

I DID THAT ONCE..

FRY. LEWIS

... I ATE A BAG OF OLESTRA CHEETOS...

I THOUGHT: "IT COULDN'T HURT"...

YOU THOUGHT?!

THERE'S A LAST TIME FOR EVERYTHING.

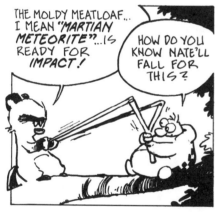

NATE MUST BE GOING THROUGH SOME SORT OF MIDLIFE CRISIS.

IT ALL STARTED WITH NORENE'S PREGNANCY.

HE'S FACING THE MOST AWESOME RESPONSIBILITY KNOWN TO MAN, AND WHAT DOES HE DO?

...BUYS A 128" MISSISSIPPI-WIDE TV!

FRYe LEWIS

THIS IS THE HAPPIEST DAY OF OUR LIVES!!!

WHEN THEY MAKE THE MOVIE OF MY LIFE, WHO DO YOU THINK SHOULD PLAY *ME?*...

ZIT.
ZIT.
ZIT.
ZIT.
ZIT.
ZIT.
ZIT.
ZIT...

FRYo LEWIS

...I'M THINKING "McCONAUGHEY" BUT I'D SETTLE FOR "COSTNER."

TONK!

MR. MAGOO'S AVAILABLE.

YOU KNOW HOW I'LL KNOW WHEN I'VE FINALLY ARRIVED?

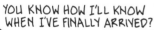

WHEN A HIGH SCHOOL MARCHING BAND IN A SMALL TOWN FORMS YOUR SILHOUETTE TO THE TUNE OF "MACARTHUR PARK."

FRY LEWIS

TNK.

WE'VE BEEN UP LATE PLOTTING WAYS TO NUKE MY SELF-ESTEEM, HAVEN'T WE?

IT KEEPS ME OFF THE STREETS.

Row 1

NOT ANOTHER AUTEUR TURN FOR THE WORSE!

NO MORE ART FILMS... I'M GOING COMMERCIAL!

OKAY... GIVE ME THE "BULLET."

"TWISTER" MEETS JANE AUSTEN!... ACTION-ADVENTURE! DECIDUOUS TO DUST! ...AUTUMN IN ALL ITS GRUESOME POWER!

AUTUMN..?

I'M CALLING IT...

...TWITTER.

FRY. LEWIS

Row 2

SPIELBERG-BOY, NOBODY'S GONNA WANT TO SEE A NATURE-THRILLER ABOUT AUTUMN.

WAIT'LL YOU SEE THE SPECIAL EFFECTS!...

FRY. LEWIS

...'SCUSE ME...

FELLAS, WHEN YOU CRASH INTO THE GROUND... I'M NOT FEELING THE PAIN!!!...

"SPECIAL EFFECTS"?

GRAVITY.

...TAKE IT FROM THE TOP!

Row 3

DON'T YOU THINK THE TRUTH OF HOW WE ADAPT TO SEASONAL CHANGE IS MORE INTERESTING THAN YOUR HIGH-TECH "ODE TO AUTUMN"?

"THE TRUTH"?

WE TURN THE THERMOSTAT UP TO 80.

FRY. LEWIS

GOODBYE, DEAR FRIEND!

PARTING IS SUCH SWEET SORROW.

IT...IT SEEMS LIKE ONLY YESTERDAY I WAS FROLICKING IN YOUR MIDST... CAUGHT IN YOUR COOL EMBRACE...≷SNIFF≷

THERE, THERE, BUBBA...

FRY & LEWIS

...WINTERIZING THE POOL IS TRAUMATIC FOR US ALL.

CAN WE GO?... THE SMELL OF CHLORINE JUST BRINGS BACK THE MEMORIES.

LOOK AT PLUSHIE! ≷SIGH≷

HEY, HE'S JUST CATCHING A FEW CATHODE RAYS!

OH, *RIGHT!*... TURNING HIS *BRAIN* INTO A *MASS* OF *GELATINOUS GOO* STARVED FOR STIMULATION, *FORCED TO TURN IN ON ITSELF UNTIL NOTHING* *REMAINS!!*

BOINK!

BOING!

FRY & LEWIS

..OOOING..OOOING.. OOING..OING...

RELAX, HE'S JUST GETTING STARTED...

PLUSHIE... YOU KNOW, SOMEDAY WE ALL PASS INTO THE *GREAT BEYOND*...

IOWA?

FRYcLEWIS

NO, JUST... *BEYOND THE INTERSECTION BETWEEN PHYSICAL AND METAPHYSICAL!*

ISN'T THAT RIGHT OUTSIDE CEDAR RAPIDS?

NO, NO, *NO!*...IT'S OUR *FINAL REST STOP ON THE HIGHWAY OF LIFE!!*

OH, I SEE...

I HOPE THERE'S A *STUCKEY'S!*

MMMM... NUT LOGS!

SO... *DISNEY* BOUGHT *CAP CITIES*... AND CAP CITIES OWNED *ABC*... SO NOW DISNEY OWNS...

EVERYTHING.

EVERYTHING?! OH, FOR *HEAVEN'S SAKE!*

THEY OWN *THAT*, TOO...

FRYc LEWIS

NOT ANOTHER THEME PARK?!!

PEOPLE ARE JUST DYING TO GET IN.

LUBY, WHEN I PEER INTO YOUR EYES, I SEE TWIN *LIMPID POOLS*, BECKONING ...AND...

...REFLECTING.. UH...

...HMM...

(WATER PIK)

ZZZ

SOME FOLKS JUST CAN'T TAKE A COMPLIMENT.

FRY.
LEWIS

VERNE, D'YA EVER GET THE FEELING FEMALES WANT SOMETHING FROM US WE CAN'T GIVE THEM?

YOU MEAN, LIKE 5 SECONDS OF OUR UNDIVIDED ATTENTION?

EXACTLY!... AND I ONCE SPENT *7.3 SECONDS* WITH LUBY, MISSING AN ENTIRE "ENTERTAIN-MENT TONIGHT" CELEBRITY BIRTHDAY SEGMENT!

MOST GUYS WON'T GO OVER ONE, TWO TENTHS OF A SECOND *TOPS!*

YEAH! AND SHE CALLS *ME* A JERK!

FRY.
LEWIS

114

NORENE'S *REALLY* STARTING TO *SHOW!*

SHE'S LOST THE ABILITY TO VELCRO HER SHOES.

PRETTY SOON SHE'LL BE DRESSED IN THE LATEST COLEMAN-TENT FASHIONS AND SPORTING REARVIEW MIRRORS, PORT AND STARBOARD!

FRYO LEWIS

RN....

...SHE'S HAVING A *BABY*...NOT A *BUICK!*

OBJECTS IN THE FUTURE ARE BLIMPIER THAN THEY APPEAR.

NORENE'S GOT A BOOK ON *HOME DELIVERY!*

SHE'S NOT HAVING THE BABY AT THE *HOSPITAL?!*

FRYOLEWIS

IS THAT *WISE?!*

WHAT ABOUT *COMPLICATIONS?!*

WILL A *DOCTOR* BE PRESENT?!

HAVE THEY *THOUGHT THIS THROUGH?!!*

=AHEM=...'COURSE, IF THEY GO TO THE HOSPITAL, *WE* WON'T BE ABLE TO *WATCH!*

90% OF BIRTHS *ARE* ROUTINE!...

AND I *DO* HAVE EVERY EPISODE OF "ER" TAPED AND READY!

WHAT KIND OF WORLD WILL NATE 'N' NORENE'S LI'L LOVE-LUMP INHERIT?

FRENZIED? PLACID? IT'S REALLY UP TO US!

YOU'RE *RIGHT*... IT'S REALLY OUR RESPONSIBILITY TO CUT THROUGH THE CLUTTER...

FRY o LEWIS

...WELL, WE *CAN'T* GET RID OF THE *TIGER WOODS* CHANNEL!... WE'D MISS HIS NEXT ENDORSEMENT...

"TIGER PEAS"!

R.J.'s TRAIL TIPS PRESENTS...

VERNE'S FAVORITE MOTIVATIONAL BOOKS!

I WONDER... IS THERE SOMETHING FOR *ME* IN THE WORLD OF "SELF HELP"?

WHAT COLOR IS YOUR PARASITE?

VERMIN WHO RUN WITH THE WOLVES

EMBRACED BY THE LICE

I'M O.K., YOU'RE RABID

FRY o LEWIS

DADDYO... SKIP RIGHT TO "SELF-911."

HOW LONG BEFORE NATE AND NORENE GET BACK?

HOURS... THEY WENT TO THE MALL TO GET NATE SOME NEW CLOTHES.

YEAH...EVER SINCE THE PREGNANCY, NATE'S BEEN PUTTING ON SOME "SYMPATHETIC POUNDS."

TOO MUCH JUNK FOOD IF YOU ASK ME!...

...I MEAN... THIS STUFF'S *GARBAGE!*

YUP...

...AND YOU KNOW WHERE GARBAGE BELONGS!

FRY. LEWIS

DOWN THE OL' *DISPOSAL!*

NO, THANKS... I'M STUFFED!

VERNE, *LOOK!*... WHAT WOULD YOU SAY *THIS* IS FOR?

HMM... I GUESS THEY DON'T NEED THE EXTRA *WARMTH.*

WELL, I, MYSELF CAN'T STAND THE DRAFTS!

I'M *FULLY* INSULATED!

FRY. LEWIS

YOU *LIE* LIKE A *DOG!*

SEE FOR YOURSELF!

OO!... TOASTY!

BELLY- BUTTON HYDRO-STATIC LINT B-GONE

RX

I FREQUENTLY WARM MY "GOOBERS" IN THERE!

ALL THOSE IN FAVOR OF LOCKING THE TRASH TO KEEP OUT PESTS... SAY "YEA"...

YEA!

TONIGHT HOMEOWNERS ASSOCIATION MEETING

OKAY... ALL THOSE OPPOSED, SAY "NAY"...

NAY!

A LITTLE LESS REVERB ON THE NEXT VOTE.

WHA-A-A-T?

FRY. LEWIS

...AND ANOTHER THING... YOU CALL THIS "FALL FOLIAGE"?

TONIGHT HOMEOWNERS ASSOCIATION MEETING

YEAH!

YIKES!

TACKY!

THE GLARE!

FRY. LEWIS

HEY!... NICE ALBERT EINSTEIN!

IT'S BROOKE SHIELDS, YOU RUBE!

R.J. & VERNE HAVE MIGRATED TO NATE & NORENE'S ATTIC...

WHOA!... A STACK OF NEW YORKERS FROM 1953!...

EXCUSE ME!...

HIBERNATION EXPERIMENT IN PROGRESS!

WHOA!... A 30,000-WORD ARTICLE ON LINT!!

I'M OUT!...

UNCONCIOUS!!...

BUENOS NOCHES, KNOTHEAD!!!

FRY LEWIS

DO YOU GET THIS CARTOON HERE?

I'VE JUST HAD IT WITH YOUR JABBERING, VERNE!... IF WE'RE GONNA SURVIVE TOGETHER IN THIS ATTIC TILL SPRING, WE'VE GOTTA SET UP BOUNDARIES!!...

...FROM NOW ON... THIS SIDE OF THIS LINE IS MY SPACE... OVER HERE IS YOUR SPACE!!...

≈MPH≈...! ≈MMMMPHH!≈

FRY LEWIS

...PARDON?

YOUR SOCK IS IN MY SPACE.

POP!